Be Made *Perfectly* WHOLE:
BODY, SPIRIT & SOUL

Deidre Campbell-Jones

Destination Publications

© 2015 – Destination Publications
DestinationChristianBooks.com
Sylmar, CA 91342
818.581.2267

ISBN-10:1-892939-02-9
ISBN-13:978-1-892939-02-9
First Edition – Printed in the United States of America

Written by Deidre Campbell-Jones
Cover photo by Terrance C. Jones

All Rights Reserved. All information contained herein cannot be copied, duplicated or reproduced for any reason, by any means: electronic, mechanical, photocopying, recording or otherwise without permission of the author or publisher. But call, we'll give permission!

This book is lovingly dedicated to the memories of Nathaniel & Docia Hayes; Beatrice & Marshall Campbell; Amy Campbell; Patricia L. Jones and Muzetta Thrower whose love of God, commitment to Christ Jesus and devotion to His Word did not overcome the attacks of sickness, disease and illnesses that robbed them of life, but instead, allowed them each to be received by the Lord into His Glorious Kingdom.

Hosea 4:6a – "My people are destroyed for lack of knowledge..."

I know that all to whom I have dedicated this book to now look on upon all who read it hoping that you will learn and live; prosper and be in health even as your souls prosper.

Hebrews 12:1-2 – "Wherefore seeing we also are compassed about with so great a cloud of witnesses, let us lay aside every weight, and the sin which doth so easily beset us, and let us run with patience the race that is set before us,
Looking unto Jesus the author and finisher of our faith; who for the joy that was set before him endured the cross, despising the shame, and is set down at the right hand of the throne of God."

Table of Contents

1.	Jesus The Healer..............................	3
2.	God Wants You Well........................	9
3.	Believe For Healing..........................	20
4.	Receive Your Healing.......................	32
•	Workbook: Let's Get Healed..............	45
5.	Whole Body......................................	47
6.	Whole Body & Spirit........................	60
7.	Wholeness: Body, Spirit & Soul..........	63
•	Workbook: Let's Get Whole...............	69

1
Jesus, The Healer

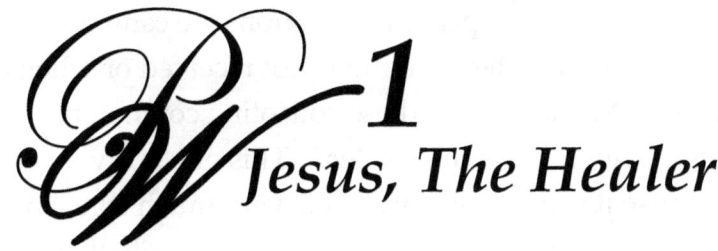

Christians often struggle with the concept of God's word being applicable today – and especially, applicable for them. Many of God's promises seem to be for "Bible times" or for someone else. We can pray for and accept healing for other people, and yet succumb to so many of our own health issues. In fact, many Christians feel a non-believer will get healed easier and faster than a Believer will – if at all. Consequently, many Christians – aided almost completely by pastors and clergy – establish their beliefs about divine, spiritual or biblical healing because of many "pulpit perspectives" and "spiritual solutions" regarding healing today. Some of these teachings include:

1. Healing is a mystery of God
2. We pray and leave the results up to the Lord
3. Who can know the mind or will of God?
4. Some healings are progressive healings
5. Just ask: Sometimes His answer is yes, no, or wait.
6. Everyone is healed, even if it's in their death that they receive perfect healing
7. His Grace is sufficient

However, many of these healing philosophies are fabricated in order to give peace in situations we cannot explain or understand when healing is not received or when a loved one dies. My favorite of these consoling comments however, is: "Only Jesus is the Healer." This one is my favorite because it is not fabricated. It is very much true, and it is the very foundation – the cornerstone if you will, that leads to God's absolute truth and very best regarding healing.

Jesus is our litmus test; the control group and the standard by which we should base all of our understanding regarding healing for today. We cannot deny that Jesus' 3 ½ years of ministry was the foundation of the Church, the foundation of Christianity and the very foundation of our Salvation. And so to separate healing from this ministry would mean separating today's church from one of the primary means by which Jesus began the Church. In fact, Jesus' full ministry consisted of three basic aspects:
1. Preaching and Teaching
2. Healing
3. Signs, Wonders & Miracles

These three aspects of Jesus' ministry were used as evangelistic tools – not only for the disciples – but for all He came across as He went about "preaching the Kingdom of God and healing the sick." Think about it – no one was a Christian – not even Jesus. And, Jesus's ministry didn't include the whole world (even though he was given to the whole world – John 3:16). Jesus was sent only to the "lost sheep of Israel." Jesus wasn't making Christians, He was making Believers in Him and he did so through preaching, teaching, healing and performing signs, wonders and miracles.

And actually, even the Passion of Jesus – His death on the cross – was comprised of all three of these categories like a final "coup de gras" compilation of His entire ministry.

Unfortunately, the understanding most Christians have about Jesus' ministry is that He died on the cross so that you and I could receive salvation. And again, while that is true, if that were the only reason, why did Jesus need the disciples? And why did He then do so many miracles and heal all who had a need? Why wouldn't He just tell the Jews He was the Son of God, make them mad and get Himself sent to the cross right away?

Well, besides fulfilling hundreds of years of prophecy, Jesus's life on earth did more than "just" provide our salvation and make the Jews mad enough to send Him to the cross.

1. Jesus came to destroy the works of the devil
2. Jesus got back the keys of death, hell and the grave
3. Jesus died on the cross for the remission of our sins

And guess what – all three include our healing!

When satan deceived Eve in the Garden of Eden and convinced her to get Adam (who was there with her – Genesis 3:6) to disobey God, that's when the works of the devil began. The enemy's work in the Garden consisted of destroying our image; stealing our blessing and killing our spirit – the spirit of God's life that the Father breathed into us Himself. These are the fundamental works of the enemy that are the basis to every reason why mankind now needs supernatural healing!

Genesis 1:26 – we (mankind) were created in the image and likeness of God: whole, healthy, complete and crowned in His perfect Glory; connected to and in communication with Him. Sickness, disease, dis-ease, pain and illness separate us from our whole image in God and our connection to God.

Genesis 1:27-28 – we (mankind) were created to be fruitful, to multiply and to replenish the earth; to subdue it and have dominion over it. Sickness, disease, dis-ease, impotence and infertility keep us from fulfilling all aspects of the blessing God. It is the enemy's way of ensuring that we remain unfruitful, depleted and controlled by the circumstances of our mind, body and the world around us.

Genesis 2:16-17 – we (mankind) were created to live for all eternity with God the Father, eating of The Tree of Life. Eating of the Tree of the Knowledge of Good and Evil caused death. And to this day, it still does. Mankind still eats of the Tree of the Knowledge of Good and Evil every day as we live life by the world's truths. Doing so causes mankind to suffer from sickness, weakness, illness, disease and dis-ease and much to the enemy's delight, all these things lead to death.

John 10:10 says, "The thief (satan) comes not but for to steal, kill and destroy. But I (Jesus) have come that you might have life and have life more abundantly." Yes, the enemy came to steal our blessing, kill our spirit and destroy our image (through any means necessary) and that includes sickness, disease and death. None of which are of God! The devil is the only one who brings sickness, disease and death. And that's why Jesus came that we might have life and life more abundantly. Perfect health is part of an abundant life!

When Jesus walked the earth in His own ministry, healing all who had a need destroyed the works of the devil. Then he taught his disciples to do the same. And as the scriptures were written for the New Testament and the early Church was established, the example was given for all of us to continue in the ministry of destroying the works of the devil. How? Through an understanding of our image; through walking in the fullness of the Genesis blessing and through a full understanding of just what our salvation provides for us. That's what Jesus' death on the cross provides for us all.

Romans 10:9-10 says, "That if thou shalt confess with thy mouth the Lord Jesus, and shalt believe in thine heart that God hath raised him from the dead, thou shalt be saved. For with the heart man believeth unto righteousness; and with the mouth confession is made unto salvation."

"Saved" in the Greek is the word "Sozo" and it means: to protect; to deliver; to HEAL; to preserve (as in long life); to save (as in from sin); to be made to do well (as in to prosper) and to be made WHOLE - complete, nothing missing, nothing lacking, nothing broken.

Most Christians only think of the confession of our salvation as being saved from sin and receiving eternal life. However, when we confess what the word of God says about our protection, we are saved through our protection. When we confess what the word of God says about our deliverance, we are saved through our deliverance. And when we confess what the word of God says about prosperity, long life, peace or wholeness or healing we are saved by receiving what the word of God says about our prosperity, long life, peace, wholeness and healing. With the mouth confession is made unto salvation! That's how God created us to function.

Our healing and wholeness is built into our salvation as Believers and therefore healing is not just for the un-believer. The non-believer (whether saved or unsaved) can receive healing and should receive healing as a part of their salvation. The Believer, whether a new "Babe in Christ" or a long-time Christian can also be healed, but should walk in complete health and wholeness as a natural part of their Christian walk. Unfortunately, many preachers and Christians say it's a lack of faith that keeps this from occurring. I say it's a lack of understanding. Christians need to understand healing as Jesus intended it to reach the lost and witness the love of Jesus as well as in their own perfect, divine and applicable healing for today – especially in relation to doctors.

Doctors are good. And having a good doctor is even better. But walking in divine health is God's best and even good doctors need God's divine best! God wants you healed, healthy and whole no matter who you are.

In Mark 6:1-7, Jesus travels to His own "country" with his disciples. There, the people who saw Him grow up amongst them were offended by Him. "Isn't this the carpenter, the son of Mary, the brothers of James, Joses, Juda and Simon? Aren't not His sisters here with us?" They thought they knew Jesus and were offended by His ministry. And as a result, Jesus could do no great miracles there and marveled at their unbelief.

Offense and unbelief will keep you in sickness and oppression. If you are offended by the message of healing; if you are offended by my message of healing that differs from what you've already heard, or if you simply do not believe in healing, you will not be healed. The good news is, you can be healed with just a little bit of belief and mustard seed faith!

2
God Wants You Well

Healing has a heartbeat. It's alive. Healing is the life of Christ that is transferred through the Spirit of God – to quicken that which is sick, weak or dying. To receive healing, you must receive that heartbeat of God. Your heart must beat in time with the truth of God's healing desires for you.

You can walk in perfect health when you understand God's heart for healing today and more importantly, His heart for healing you.

You have a physical heart that beats regularly and consistently when you are healthy and it pumps life generating blood throughout all the parts of your body. Your spirit has a heart that beats regularly and consistently when you are feeding it from the word of God so that it can pump love generated power and truth to every area of your life. But we need to treat our spiritual heart in the same manner as we treat our physical heart.

- Do you have to decide whether or not you believe your heart is beating?
- Do you question whether your heart is meant to beat or not?
- Do you doubt whether a beating heart is meant for you?

- Do you have to beg God to keep your heart beating every day?
- And finally, do you recognize the feel of your heart beat or do you reject it?

Of course the answer is "no" to all of these statements regarding our physical, natural heart. But this is exactly what we do when it comes to understanding whether or not God wants you healed. We spend much time deciding whether or not we believe in healing. We question whether or not healing is meant for us. We doubt whether we will get healed or keep a healing – especially if we've begged God for it. And in fact, most healing prayers, or cries in the midst of our pain, sickness or distress is a deep pleading and begging for God to have mercy upon us and healing. And finally, when we do hear a sermon or teaching on healing, we generally don't know enough about God or His word to really even recognize His true desire for us to be healed and therefore, we often reject it. However, that rejection is actually a defense mechanism to protect our hearts from being hurt if indeed we do not receive God's healing.

So when it comes to the heartbeat of healing, the first step is to realize that God's heart for you is to be healed. You need to recognize the sound of God's heart beat for you: it sounds like healing and health. No matter what your name is, when you were born, what denomination you are or even if you feel you contributed to your poor health yourself – God loves you so much and it breaks His heart when you are not well. God's heart for you does not beat steady or strong when you are not in health. That's why God's heart for you is for you to be in good health (3 John 1:2).

Believing God's heart for your healing means to have faith that God wants you healed and to believe that there are no limitations, no qualifications, no prerequisites and no loopholes that pertain to your healing. Sin, error, judgment, unforgiveness and ignorance (as in God is trying to teach you something) are in no way connected to whether or not you get healed and walk in divine spiritual health. Your good deeds, good behavior, righteousness, prayer life, biblical study habits or love towards your neighbor have no negative affect on whether or not you get healed or walk in divine spiritual health. Belief and Faith are the only determining factors towards your healing. But you are still not excluded if you feel like "you don't have enough faith."

The good news is – I do. The even better news, or the "too-good-to-be-true" news about healing is the word of God itself. Why? Because the Gospel of Jesus Christ is the "too-good-to-be-true" news of the Word of God. That's what "gospel" means. And, Romans 10:13-17 talks about your faith – especially in regard to what you believe in the word of God. Verse 17 says faith comes from hearing and hearing from the word of God. But before that it says, how can you hear without a preacher? Well, I am just that preacher to help you hear that God really does want you healed and whole.

But first – are you saved? Have you confessed with your mouth the Lord Jesus and believed in your heart that God raised Him from the dead? If your answer is "no" or you're "not sure," then take the time to pray now. It only takes a brief prayer (just a few seconds) to secure an eternity with God through Jesus Christ. You don't need salvation to be healed, but once you are saved, then wholeness, prosperity and so much more are yours as well!

And so, if you did just say that prayer for the first time, or if your answer was "yes" you have confessed Jesus as your Lord and Savior, then Romans 10:9 and 13 says – YOU ARE SAVED! And, here's the best part – your salvation includes many instant benefits (Psalm 103:2), that are inherent in the very definition of the word "saved."

Again, the Greek word "sozo" means: to protect, to deliver, to **HEAL**, to preserver (as in long life), to save (…from sin, as in eternal life), to make to do well (as in to prosper) and to be made whole – nothing missing, nothing, lacking, nothing broken – amen, that's awesome! So, when Romans 10:13 says, "For whosoever shall call upon the name of the Lord shall be saved," that means whoever calls upon the name of Jesus will be protected, or delivered, or **HEALED,** or preserved, or saved from sin, or prospered, or perfected. Wow…!

- But Romans 10:14 says, "How then shall they call on him in whom they have not believed?"
- And Romans 10:14 also says, "And how shall they believe in him of whom they have not heard?
- And also, "How shall they hear without a preacher?"

You need a pastor or a preacher to preach the word of God so that you can hear the Word of God. Then when you hear the TRUE word of God you will believe the Word of God. Well, Romans 10:15 is the verse God used to first call me into the ministry to be a minister, preacher and pastor: "And how shall they preach, except they be sent? As it is written, How beautiful are the feet of them that preach the gospel of peace, and bring glad tidings of good things!"

Ch. 2 – God Wants You Well

And so I admonish you, adjure you and beseech you – do not be as Romans 10:16 says, "But they have not all obeyed the gospel. For Esaias saith, Lord, who hath believed our report?" Please believe this report because Romans 10:17 says, "So then faith cometh by hearing, and hearing by the word of God."

Your faith for healing comes when you hear and hear and keep on hearing the word of God. And before you disqualify yourself because you are reading this, just know, Romans 10:15, the verse that called me into the ministry is a New Testament quote of the Old Testament scripture in Isaiah 52:7 which says, "How beautiful upon the mountains are the feet of him that bringeth good tidings, that publisheth peace; that bringeth good tidings of good, that publisheth salvation; that saith unto Zion, Thy God reigneth!" And so I am speaking it, writing it and publishing it for the world to hear: MY GOD REIGNS AND HE WANTS YOU HEALED!

The word of God is full of proof regarding your healing:
- Isaiah 53:5 – "He was wounded for our transgressions, he was bruised for our iniquities: the chastisement of our peace was upon him; and with his stripes **WE ARE HEALED.**"
- Psalm 30:2 – "O LORD my God, I cried unto thee, and thou hast **HEALED** me."
- Psalm 103:2-3 – "Bless the LORD, O my soul, and forget not all his benefits: Who forgiveth all thine iniquities; who **HEALS ALL THY DISEASES;**"
- Psalm 107:20 – "He sent his word, and **HEALED** them, and delivered them from their destructions."
- Psalm 147:3 – "[The Lord] He **HEALS** the broken in heart, and bindeth up their wounds."

- Proverbs 4:20-22 – "My son, attend to **my words**; incline thine ear unto my sayings. Let them not depart from thine eyes; keep them in the midst of thine heart, for they **are life** unto those that find them, and **HEALTH** to all their flesh."
- Proverbs 16:24 – "Pleasant words are as an honeycomb, sweet to the soul, and **HEALTH** to the bones."
- Malachi 4:2 – "But unto you that fear my name shall the Sun of righteousness arise with **HEALING** in his wings; and ye shall go forth, and grow up as calves of the stall."
- Matthew 4:23-24 – "And Jesus went about all Galilee, teaching in their synagogues, and preaching the gospel of the kingdom, and **HEALING** all manner of sickness and all manner of disease among the people. And his fame went throughout all Syria: and they brought unto him all sick people that were taken with divers diseases and torments, and those which were possessed with devils, and those which were lunatic, and those that had the palsy; and **HE HEALED THEM**."
- Matthew 8:16-17 – "When the even was come, they brought unto him many that were possessed with devils: and he cast out the spirits with his word, and **HEALED ALL** that were sick: That it might be fulfilled which was spoken by Esaias the prophet, saying, **Himself took our infirmities, and bare our sicknesses**."
- Matthew 9:35 – "And Jesus went about all the cities and villages, teaching in their synagogues, and preaching the gospel of the kingdom, and **HEALING every sickness and every disease** among the people."
- Matthew 12:15 – "But when Jesus knew it, he withdrew himself from thence: and great multitudes followed him, and **he HEALED them all**;"

- Matthew 14:14 – "And Jesus went forth, and saw a great multitude, and was moved with compassion toward them, and he **HEALED** their sick."
- Matthew 15:30 – "And great multitudes came unto him, having with them those that were lame, blind, dumb, maimed, and many others, and cast them down at Jesus' feet; and he **HEALED** them:"
- Mark 1:32-34 – "And at even, when the sun did set, they brought unto him all that were diseased, and them that were possessed with devils. And all the city was gathered together at the door. And he **HEALED** many that were sick of divers diseases, and cast out many devils; and suffered not the devils to speak, because they knew him."
- Mark 16:17-18 – "And these signs shall follow them that believe; In my name shall they cast out devils; they shall speak with new tongues; They shall take up serpents; and if they drink any deadly thing, it shall not hurt them; **they shall lay hands on the sick, and they shall recover.**"
- Luke 4:18-19 – "The Spirit of the Lord is upon me, because he hath anointed me to preach the gospel to the poor; he hath sent me to **HEAL the brokenhearted**, to preach deliverance to the captives, and recovering of sight to the blind, to set at liberty them that are bruised, To preach the acceptable year of the Lord."
- Luke 4:40 – "Now when the sun was setting, all they that had any sick with divers diseases brought them unto him; and he laid his hands on every one of them, and **HEALED** them."
- Luke 5:17 – "And it came to pass on a certain day, as he was teaching, that there were Pharisees and doctors of the law sitting by, which were come out of every town of

Galilee, and Judaea, and Jerusalem: and the **power of the Lord was present to HEAL them.**"

- Luke 6:17-19 – "And he came down with them, and stood in the plain, and the company of his disciples, and a great multitude of people out of all Judaea and Jerusalem, and from the sea coast of Tyre and Sidon, which came to hear him, and to be healed of their diseases; And they that were vexed with unclean spirits: **and they were HEALED.** And the whole multitude sought to touch him: for there went virtue out of him, and **HEALED** them all."
- Luke 9:2 & 6 – "And he sent them to preach the kingdom of God, and **to heal the sick.** And they departed, and went through the towns, preaching the gospel, and **HEALING everywhere**"
- Luke 9:11 – "And the people, when they knew it, followed him: and he received them, and spake unto them of the kingdom of God, and **HEALED them that had need of healing.**"
- John 4:47 – "When he heard that Jesus was come out of Judaea into Galilee, he went unto him, and besought him that he would come down, and **heal** his son: for he was at the point of death." (Verse 50: Jesus says, "Go thy way, **thy son liveth**. And the man believed the word Jesus had spoken unto him.")
- Acts 3:11 (Peter and John see a lame man by the Temple and Peter tells him "silver and gold have I none, but such that I have I give unto you; **Arise and walk.**") Verse 11: "And as the lame man which was **HEALED** held Peter and John, all the people ran together unto them in the porch that is called Solomon's, greatly wondering."
- Acts 5:16 – "There came also a multitude out of the cities round about unto Jerusalem, bringing sick folks, and

them which were vexed with unclean spirits: and they were **HEALED every one.**"
- Acts 8:7-8 – "For unclean spirits, crying with loud voice, came out of many that were possessed with them: and many taken with palsies, and that were lame, were **HEALED.** And there was great joy in that city."
- Acts 10:38 – "God anointed Jesus of Nazareth with the Holy Ghost and with power: who went about doing good, and **HEALING all that were oppressed of the devil**; for God was with him."
- Acts 14:9-10 – "The same heard Paul speak: who stedfastly beholding him, and perceiving that **he had faith to be healed,** Said with a loud voice, **Stand upright on thy feet. And he leaped and walked.**"
- Acts 28:8-9 – "And it came to pass, that the father of Publius lay sick of a fever and of a bloody flux: to whom Paul entered in, and prayed, and laid his hands on him, and **HEALED** him. So when this was done, others also, which had diseases in the island, came, and were **HEALED:**"
- James 5:16 – "Confess your faults one to another, and pray one for another, that **ye may be HEALED.** The effectual fervent prayer of a righteous man availeth much."
- 3 John 1:2 – "Beloved, I wish above all that you would prosper, and **BE IN HEALTH** even as your soul prospers."
- 1 Peter 2:24 – "Who his own self bare our sins in his own body on the tree, that we, being dead to sins, should live unto righteousness: by whose stripes **YOU WERE HEALED.**

Do you see? God wants you healed. Jesus healed all who had a need. He taught the disciples to heal. And then the Apostles healed. Peter and Paul both healed and Jesus gave all believers the ability to heal and be healed. Above all else, our heavenly Father wants you to prosper and be in health even as your soul prospers. Giving you all these verses on healing is for the prosperity of your soul!

Do you want to be healed? Do you want to walk in health? Do you want to receive the promises of healing God has given you in His word? Do you want to receive of the healing found in God's word? Of course we instinctively say yes, but sometimes we are afraid to be healed. The man by the pool of Bethesda gave Jesus excuses. Don't let your words keep you from being healed! The power of healing – in fact, the very power of your own life is in your own mouth.

Proverbs 18:21 – "Death and life are in the power of the tongue: and they that love it shall eat the fruit thereof.

I'm sure many of us would love it if this verse meant there was a fruit that we could put under our tongue like some holistic medicine and it would bring life, health and healing to our bodies. But the truth is, God has given us all power over our lives through what we say. And what we say is determined by what we believe. And what we believe is determined by the word of God that we read, hear and know.

Everything we speak is a direct result of what is abundant in our hearts. (Luke 6:45) What we believe is stored up in our hearts like a treasure and you can bring forth the good treasure of healing in your life through your own words!

3
Believe For Healing

Do you want to be free from the bondage of sickness, pain or disease? John 8:32 says, "And ye shall know the truth, and the truth shall make you free." The word of God is truth and Jesus is the Way, the TRUTH and the Life. When you know the truth you know Jesus and Jesus will set you free from the bondage of sickness, pain and disease. God sent His word (of Truth) to heal (the lies) of the enemy!

It is imperative that you know, that you know, that you know what God thinks about your health and healing so that you can believe in your own healing! Both Proverbs 3:3 and 7:3 say that the word of God's teaching should be written upon the tablet of our hearts. The word of God is stored in our hearts as belief. But Luke 8:12 says that the enemy is ready to take away the word from our hearts so that we do NOT believe and get saved!

That means when we believe the word of God in our hearts we can be saved or "sozoed" (so to speak).
- The word of truth that we **know** sets us free and <u>protects</u> us.
- The word of truth that we **know** sets us free and <u>delivers</u> us.
- The word of truth that we **know** sets us free and <u>preserves</u> us.
- The word of truth we **know** sets us free and <u>saves us from sin</u>
- The word of truth we **know** sets us free and <u>gives abundant life</u>
- The word of truth we **know** sets us free and <u>makes us whole</u>

- The word of truth that we **know** sets us free and **HEALS** us!

Your healing and your divine health is first dependent upon the word that you hear (Romans 10:14.) Your healing and divine health is then dependent upon the word you hear that you know to be true. (John 8:38). Then, your healing and divine health is dependent upon the word that you know to be true that you believe in your heart. (Luke 8:12). And finally, your healing and divine health is dependent upon the word you believe in your heart that you speak with your mouth. (Proverbs 18:21)

Here are the five steps to receiving your healing and taking power over your health:

1. Hear it.
2. Know it.
3. Believe it.
4. Speak it.
5. And do not doubt it!

> **Mark 11:23-24 – "For verily I say unto you, That whosoever shall say unto this mountain, Be thou removed, and be thou cast into the sea; and shall not doubt in his heart, but shall believe that those things which he saith shall come to pass; he shall have whatsoever he saith. Therefore I say unto you, What things soever ye desire, when ye pray, believe that ye receive them, and ye shall have them."**

HEAR THE WORD: Everyday, you should go over these scriptures regarding healing and read them out loud first thing in the morning until you…

KNOW THE WORD: Once you know the word enough that the enemy cannot steal the word from your heart that is when your freedom is about to begin because you will then…

BELIEVE THE WORD: Believing the word of God means having faith IN God and having the God kind of faith as Jesus said in Mark 11:22. And believing the word is what gives you the power and the authority to…

SPEAK THE WORD: But speaking the word isn't enough. You've got to speak the word continuously with the same power, authority and belief in the Word so that you…

DO NOT DOUBT THE WORD: The enemy will try to continue the lie! That's what he does – that's who he is. The devil is a liar; he is the father of lies and there is no truth in him.

Every pain you feel is a lie. Every doctor's report for every single disease is a report of facts, not truth. Every headache is a lie. Every improper blood pressure level, sugar count or heart rate is a lie. And every diagnosis for every ailment, mental illness, condition or sickness is again a factual report that is based upon a lie and not the truth.

Sickness, pain, disease and dis-ease are not of God – they are of the devil and the symptoms of them are lies that the enemy wants you to believe rather than the truth of God!

If you're wondering how I can possibly say that – well, it's based upon the revelation I had regarding Isaiah 53:5 and 1 Peter 2:24. In the book of Isaiah, the prophecy of Jesus' coming says that we ARE healed – even though Jesus had not yet died on the cross for our healing. And in 1 Peter it says were WERE healed, meaning once Jesus came, he purchased our healing on the cross for all of us.

So then, here we are more than 2000 years past Jesus' death and resurrection and the word of God still stands that by His stripes we WERE healed. How can we be healed before we are even born? Or before we are even born again? Or before we are even sick?

Jesus purchased our healing for us with His own blood. Healing is the truth. Our divine health is the truth. Our peace of mind is truth! Therefore, anything that differs from that means the devil is trying to steal our health, steal our healing and steal what is rightfully ours. Healing IS the "children's bread." If you believe on Jesus by faith you are the seed of Abraham and a child of God by faith. We have been given the spirit of adoption, made co-heirs to Jesus and through Jesus we have been redeemed from the curse of the law, including all manner of sickness, disease and death! (Galatians 3:6-14)

Therefore every symptom; every sneeze; every pain; every ache, every disease and every dis-ease; every illness, sickness, weakness, hindrance and problem that keeps you or your body from functioning decently and in order, whole and complete, healthy and in perfect peace is a flat out, undeniable, totally "rebukable" lie of the devil himself! And you have the right, the authority and the power to be healed in Jesus' name and to continue walking in divine health too.

And since your sickness, disease, dis-ease, illness, weakness or hindrance is a lie of the devil, you don't have to accept any Christian based justifications regarding your health either. They are true but are not prerequisites to your healing!

- God isn't trying to teach you anything through sickness
- God isn't trying to get your attention through disease
- God isn't waiting for you to forgive anyone to be healed
- God isn't waiting for you to give to anyone to be whole

- God isn't picking and choosing who gets healed
- God isn't going to give you a "progressive" healing
- God isn't saying wait for your healing
- God isn't saying no to your healing

In fact, all of God promises "in him are yea, and in him Amen, unto the glory of God by us." (2 Corinthians 1:20) And just so you are sure; "yea" means "yes" and "Amen" means "let it be." When God gives a promise, he gives it as a "yes" and when we receive that promise – by hearing it, knowing it and believing it – we are essentially saying, "let it be." We are the ones who say "amen" to all of God's promises and God says "yes" simply by giving them.

And so, because all things work together for the good of them who love the Lord and are the called according to His purpose [Romans 8:28], then if you learn something while you're sick or you turn your attention to God while you're sick, or you think to forgive or think to give then it's because what the devil meant for evil, God used for good.

God doesn't make you sick in order to do any of those things; but He can use your sickness to do those things. Still – that won't keep you from getting healed! Sometimes we pick and choose for ourselves whether or not we get healed by our own misconceptions.

Some people think a headache is too small to ask God healing for; and sometimes people think cancer, Aids or a missing limb is too "hard" for God. Oh, we don't think it or say it out loud, but we certainly pray for those circumstances from the perspective of whether or not we believe God can or will do it. But Jeremiah 32:27 says nothing is too hard for God and therefore NOTHING is impossible WITH God!

The same is true for "progressive" healings. Truthfully, there really isn't any case of healing that was "progressive" or where Jesus said – just keep the faith and keep asking and you never know – you may see your healing next week, next month or next year because it will be a progressive healing.

The only biblical account that makes people teach a "progressive" healing is regarding the blind man in Mark 8. But Jesus had to remove that man from his lack of faith for his healing to progress as effectively it needed to.

No, the only thing progressive about a true healing is the progressive faith we use to ultimately manifest that healing! In fact, let me be bold enough to say:

WE ARE OUR OWN LIMITATION TO HEALING AND DIVINE HEALTH

Now then, we have to dispel one more major myth around your healing and divine health: whether or not God will. You see, many Christians do not know that we are already blessed and that God's promises are already ours. Many Christians are still living in the "shall be," or "will be" and "if's" of the word of God.

But every last one of those "shall-be-will-be-if's" are from before Jesus's death, burial, resurrection and ascension into heaven. After Jesus went to the cross, all of God's promises are "have, has and did" – even if it reads like "shall-be-will-be-if." Think of it this way: you HAVE received your salvation, right? Then you HAVE been given your protection, deliverance,, preservation, eternal life, prosperity, wholeness, peace and HEALING. Now let's receive it!

The five steps listed previously: hear it; know it; speak it; believe it and do not doubt it are ways in which we can receive and maintain our own divine health. But the bible lists two ways in which we can receive divine healing – especially if our faith is not strong enough to manifest it on our own. And sometimes, that is the case. Praying for your own healing can sometimes take time, or seem to back fire or not work. That's because we can feel our own pain, and we focus on the pain, the sickness or the symptom instead of focusing on using the faith that will wipe out that pain, sickness or symptom. Sometimes it takes time to build up our own faith for our own healing. But that is not a "progressive" healing – that is progressive faith!

Mark 16:17-18 – "And these signs shall follow them that believe; In my name shall they cast out devils; they shall speak with new tongues; They shall take up serpents; and if they drink any deadly thing, it shall not hurt them; they shall lay hands on the sick, and they shall recover."

Believers can and should lay hands on one another if we are sick and EXPECT that that will recover. Oh, my Beloved – it just irks my spirit when Christians are told to just pray and let God worry about the results. I think this came about as a way of comforting one another when someone was prayed for and healing did not happen.

Yes, only Jesus can result a healing, but I believe if you are a Believer and feel you don't have enough faith to expect that whoever you lay hands on shall recover, then you still don't know how to use the faith to pray for healing in the first place. When the bible speaks of "little" faith, it's referring to how much you use and not how much you have. Romans 12:3 says every man is given THE measure of faith. You have faith!

Jesus said, "These are the signs that WILL follow those who believe..." and I say that applies not just to those who believe in Him because many do believe in Jesus but most certainly do not see healing at their own hands. Instead, we must also believe that this word of scripture is also true. We must believe that Believers can lay hands on the sick and they shall recover. That means we can have hands laid upon us, we can lay hands on others and I dare you to grow enough in faith that you lay hands on yourself and expect results as well!

Now then, James 5:14-15 says, "Is any sick among you? Let him call for the elders of the church; and let them pray over him, anointing him with oil in the name of the Lord: And the prayer of faith shall save the sick, and the Lord shall raise him up; and if he have committed sins, they shall be forgiven him."

The Elders of your church and my church – technically of The Church – *should* be mature enough in their faith and in THEIR measure of faith that they can anoint the sick among their congregations, pray for them in the name of Jesus and expect that they will be raised up and healed. What a wonderful ministry for the elders of a congregation! And think of the evangelistic tool this would provide as well. If the Elder went to the home of someone with an unbelieving child or relative who was sick and they prayed over them, that person would receive salvation as well as healing!

But you don't have to be an Elder to pray the prayer of faith. A prayer of faith is one that is fully confident and expectant that the prayer will manifest exactly as the word of God says that it will – no doubt, nothing wavering, done deal! That is how you use great faith – when you pray (in faith), just believe you have already received and do not doubt it one bit!

Here's a mini-teaching: Many Christians (and leaders) erroneously believe that James 5:14-15 means if you do have sin in your life then you can't get healed. Or that the sin in your life is what caused the sickness – like a punishment from God for walking in sin. Nope, God isn't punishing anyone with sickness of any kind, for any reason. Jesus didn't stop anyone – not one person in the multitudes – and ask if they had sin in their life before He healed them. Nor did He separate those who had forgiven and those who hadn't.

Jesus came to destroy the works of the devil and in His ministry He healed those who were oppressed of the devil. Sickness is of the devil and so is sin! And so doesn't it make sense then that if you pray for the unbeliever who has sin in their life that the sickness and the sin get dealt with together? Praying for the sick unbeliever will not only bring about healing but salvation too! That's why Jesus said, "Which is easier to say; your sins are forgiven or arise and walk!"

Having an Elder anoint you with oil and pray for you when you are sick will work. My father is Steward President in the AME Church, and that's not necessarily a denomination that practices having the elders anoint with oil and pray for the sick. But there was a time when he was 79 years old that while visiting him my body became wracked with the most excruciating pain. I was so seized with pain that breathing was difficult but I prayed, cried and spoke scripture over my body for hours – all to no avail. Finally, I gathered enough energy and voice to call in my father and ask him to anoint my back with oil and pray for me. He did it, but really only out of concern for me. But his prayer gained momentum and within 15 minutes that pain was gone and I was finally sleeping peacefully. The prayers of the Elders works in Jesus' name!

Now, our original list of ways in which to be healed consists of five things, and I've just added the two others: Laying hands on one another; and having an Elder anoint you with oil and pray. But like God Himself says, for example, that there are 7 things that He hates, yea even eight, and so I'm going to do the same and add an eighth example of how we can gain our own healing. This one however, is a bit more controversial, but it is also an example of not only receiving healing but maintaining our divine health as well as an answer to why we get sick, weak or die in the first place.

Let me deliver to you the revelation of Communion that I have received just as Paul said to the Church in Corinth:

1 Corinthians 11:23-30 says, "For I have received of the Lord that which also I delivered unto you, That the Lord Jesus the same night in which he was betrayed took bread: And when he had given thanks, he brake it, and said, Take, eat: this is my body, which is broken for you: this do in remembrance of me. After the same manner also he took the cup, when he had supped, saying, This cup is the new testament in my blood: this do ye, as oft as ye drink it, in remembrance of me. For as often as ye eat this bread, and drink this cup, ye do show the Lord's death till he come. Wherefore whosoever shall eat this bread, and drink this cup of the Lord, unworthily, shall be guilty of the body and blood of the Lord. But let a man examine himself, and so let him eat of that bread, and drink of that cup. For he that eateth and drinketh unworthily, eateth and drinketh damnation to himself, not discerning the Lord's body. For this cause many are weak and sickly among you, and many sleep."

Many have taught, learned and believe that "eating or drinking unworthily" means having some unresolved issue while you are taking communion – such as having sin in your life or having something against your brother or someone having something against you. First, God will never turn away a person who has sin in their life who comes to His Holy Communion – especially if they believe that the cup is the blood of the New Testament which was shed for the remission of their sin. As soon as they believe that and take that cup it's like confessing Jesus as their Lord and Savior who saves us all from sin – the same sin that the cup of the blood of the New Testament puts into remission for all of us!

I say let every unbeliever, sinner and person with unforgiveness in their heart take communion. If we ever taught communion correctly and thoroughly – especially with the truth of Jesus' blood and His forgiveness for us through the shedding of His blood, churches throughout the world would probably bring so many people to salvation through communion alone! So, that is not what this verse is saying.

And the thought pertaining to "having ought against someone or someone having ought against you" is found in Matthew 5:23-24 and refers to your tithe and offering before the altar of the church: "Therefore if thou bring thy gift to the altar, and there rememberest that thy brother hath ought against thee; Leave there thy gift before the altar, and go thy way; first be reconciled to thy brother, and then come and offer thy gift." So, this verse has nothing to do with reconciling before taking communion either, but how many still give offerings with unresolved issues in their lives?

If we made people ask for forgiveness before giving in church, many congregations would probably go bankrupt!

In truth, the way in which we eat or drink unworthily is found in the verse of text itself: "For he who eats and drinks unworthily, brings damnation unto himself, **not discerning the Lord's body."**

When we do not discern what Jesus' body did for us on the cross, we eat and drink unworthily, and the damnation we bring upon ourselves is the very thing that Jesus' death on the cross was intended to *save* us from – in particular, our health. Why? Because the end of that text says, "For *this* cause many are weak and sickly and sleep among you." I add the emphasis on the word "this" because "this" is a definitive word. This is the cause. This is not one of the causes – this is the cause for many of our weakness or infirmities (that's what infirmities means), and our sicknesses, and all other manner of disease and/or dis-ease (mental distress and illness) that lead to death in a Believer – because Jesus says that Believers do not die, we fall asleep in the Lord.

Jesus came that we might have life and have it more abundantly (John 10:10) and his sacrifice on the cross was (in part) for our healing. Remember, 1 Peter 2:24 says, "By His stripes we were healed." It must be a trick of the devil that we as Believers will remember that Jesus' blood is for the remission of our sin, before we remember that Jesus was beaten and bruised for our infirmities as well as our iniquities.

Yes, the word says to take communion in remembrance of Jesus' death until His return. But in remembering his death we must not only remember His blood for the remission of our sin, but also the healing for our bodies that was given to us *through* His death on the cross! Taking communion in remembrance of Jesus' body then is a way to receive all that His body provides for us in healing and in divine health.

Yes, it's controversial to say that you can receive your healing through communion. But it was controversial for Jesus to heal on the Sabbath Day. The Scribes and Pharisees weren't at all astonished at the miracles – their hearts were so hardened that they were only accusatory over the structure and deliverance of those miracles. But do you think any of those people who were healed on the Sabbath gave back their miracle because they were not supposed to have been healed on the Sabbath? Of course not!

It is not the physical act of communion that can bring about your healing. It is the act of remembering what the Lord's body has provided for you in terms of your healing and the act of faith associated with it. Therefore, do not let the controversy around the healing properties of Holy Communion keep you from receiving your divine healing any way that you have the faith to receive it! Let Jesus say to you the same as He said to the two blind men in Matthew 9:29, "According to YOUR faith, be it unto you."

So let's recap our seven, yea even eight biblical ways in which believers can receive healing and maintain their divine health. It's all a matter of what you have the faith for. It is my desire to build your faith to the degree that any of these work:

1. Hear it
2. Know it
3. Believe it
4. Speak it
5. Do not doubt it
6. Lay hands on it
7. Have the Elders pray for it
8. Take Communion for it

4
Receive Your Healing

Now, you might be reminding me that the first five in our list of eight ways to believe for healing, are actually a group of one way and therefore the recalculated list would actually be a total of only four ways in which a Believer can receive and maintain divine healing and health.

Yes, if you are only going to take your healing into your own hands, then that it true. It is a lifestyle of living that hears the word, knows the truth of that word, believes that word, speaks it and does not doubt it consistently that will bring about your healing.

It is hard work to use any of these methods. It is a process. The enemy will continually lie to you about whether or not "God will heal you." Your body will betray you and symptoms are stubborn to leave. Your mouth will betray you and you will find yourself speaking against your own healing without realizing it. And the world will try to discourage you through doctors' reports, commercials for medications and comments from well-meaning friends and family.

The enemy won't make it easy however Jesus used each of these ways in His own Earthly healing ministry as individual examples of how to receive healing for ourselves.

HEAR IT

So let's start with the obvious. You know that you can attend an event, hear the right message on a Sunday morning, or watch a Christian Television program on healing and just through the hearing of the word you will find yourself healed. The Spirit of the Lord that was present for the Pharisees to be healed in Luke 15:17 will transcend time and space and will be present for your healing the same in a new Sunday sermon delivered by your Pastor as in an 5 year old You Tube video from an empowered preacher out of Arizona, Singapore, Canada or Sylmar, California.

In Matthew 12:13 Jesus said to the man with the withered hand, "stretch forth your hand." And when the man did, it was restored whole like the other one. Nowhere does it say that Jesus touched the man, laid hands on him or anointed him. Simply in hearing the words of Jesus the man was healed. When you hear with the ears of faith you too can be healed from simply hearing the word of God.

There is another way in which you can be healed from hearing the word of God. Go back to the list of scriptures I've written for you and read them over and over again, out loud. Let your own ears hear your own mouth speaking the word of God.

Romans 10:17 says faith comes by hearing and hearing by the word of God. So let your faith come by hearing and hearing and continuing to hear your own mouth speaking the word of God. It worked for Dodi Osteen, Joel Osteen's mother and it can work for you too when you mix the scriptures with faith. She continues to speak the scriptures like daily medication and her health has been maintained.

KNOW IT

Now, maybe you don't belong to church where the Pastor will preach about healing in a manner that stirs up your faith for healing. And maybe you're too ill to get to an event where the preacher will do that also. And maybe you don't receive the kind of Christian Television channels that broadcast dynamic healing services. But you are reading this book now. And as you read over the healing scriptures listed, instead of only reading them out loud you can also study them. Pray to receive the revelation of them so that you can know the absolute truth of each verse and Jesus, the Healer.

Or better yet read them directly from your bible. You can read the scriptures and stories about healing in the bible with faith and be healed by knowing the truth of what you read. No matter where you are, no matter how infirm you might be – you can know Psalm 107:20 for yourself: "He sent his word, and healed them, and delivered them from their destructions."

In Matthew 5:8-13 The Centurion soldier sent messengers to ask Jesus to heal his servant. Jesus was willing to go to his house but the Centurion said he was not worthy, but to say the word and his servant would be healed. The Centurion *knew* the authority of the word. He *knew* that Jesus walked in that kind of authority. Jesus said he had not seen so great a faith in all of Israel and as he believed so it was. The Centurion's servant was healed simply because his master knew he would be.

You can receive the same power of healing through the truths you know about healing. In fact, John 8:32 says it is the truth you *know* that will set you free…

BELIEVE IT

Now before you point out that the healing of the Centurion soldier's servant was a healing for someone else and not the soldier himself, let me remind you of the woman with the issue of blood. Her move of faith for her healing – her own healing – encompasses both "hearing," "knowing" and "believing" as well as "speaking!"

Matthew 9:20-21 "And, behold, a woman, which was diseased with an issue of blood twelve years, came behind him, and touched the hem of his garment: For she said within herself, If I may but touch his garment, I shall be whole."

In the original Greek text, the phrase "For she said within herself" has a definition of the word "said" that means "kept saying." The woman with the issue of blood kept saying within herself – or to herself – "if I can touch his garment, I will be whole." Her comment has a sense of knowing. She knew that if she could get close enough to Jesus to touch his garment she would be made whole.

What did she know that initiated her diligence to keep speaking that one thing over and over to herself? Mark's version of this story seems to be the same account, however his wording offers us a few clues as to what this woman knew that led to her healing.

Mark 5:27-28 "When she had heard of Jesus, came in the press behind, and touched his garment. For she said, If I may touch but his clothes, I shall be whole."

Mark tells us that this woman "heard" of Jesus. She heard something that made her believe that if she could get to Jesus she would be made whole. I am sure she may have heard the excited whispers, accounts and testimonies of all who had been healed through the ministry of this man.

That continual hearing, became belief, and her belief became faith and as she kept speaking her faith to herself, her heart kept hearing it and kept strengthening her resolve.

The Greek gives us another clue as to what this woman of faith may have heard. The word "hem" means border, edge or fringe or tassel. The hem, border, edge, fringe or tassels of the Rabbi's Talit or prayer shawl were called the "wings" in Hebrew. And in Malachi 4:2, (a Hebrew scripture our woman with the issue of blood most assuredly would have known), it says, "But unto you that fear my name shall the Sun of righteousness arise with healing in his wings; and ye shall go forth, and grow up as calves of the stall."

Our woman with the issue of blood **heard** that there was a man who was healing the sick of all manner of diseases, ailments and infirmities. And in **knowing** this scripture that said there would be healing in the wings or the tassels of the garment of the Son of Righteousness, she **believed** if she could touch the garment of Jesus, she would be made whole.

And as she pressed through the crowd, doing what she was not supposed to do; being where she was not supposed to be; going against the years of suffering and the worsening of her health and circumstances, this woman spoke to herself and kept **speaking** to herself the truth that she believed by faith. Her effort prevailed. In her persistence she did indeed touch the hem of Jesus' garment. Virtue – which is the power of His divine nature – poured out of Him and she took her healing by faith. It was not Jesus who actively and knowingly healed her – in fact, he only was aware of the healing when He felt her touch and the pull of virtue that her touch drew out from Him. Jesus turned and when he saw her He said, "Daughter, YOUR faith has made you whole."

SPEAK IT

Are you seeing the pattern now? Hebrews 11:1 says, "NOW faith is the substance of things hoped for, the evidence of things unseen." Is healing unseen? Is your health unseen? Is it difficult to see how you will be cured? Does the doctor's diagnosis keep you from seeing long life and health in your future? Faith will manifest the healing, health, good report and long life that you cannot see! Faith can see!

When four men lowered their ill friend in need of healing down through the roof of Jesus' house, He looked up and "saw their faith." When you have the faith to be healed you can see yourself well. But sometimes we are sick for so long, our hope for healing gets deferred because we can no longer see ourselves living life healed, whole and well.

If you are hoping to be healed, hoping to walk in divine health and hoping to be around to see your grandchildren grow up, and you can see it happening, then your faith is the substance of those hopes. Or rather, your faith is power that will make those hopes substantial and evident in your life!

That's what happened with the woman who had the issue of blood. She heard something; she knew something; she believed something and she kept speaking something that brought about her healing. What was that something? Faith. She heard about Jesus and that ignited her faith. She mixed what she heard with what she knew and it became belief – a belief that manifested into faith as she spoke it and kept speaking it and acted upon what she was speaking! You see, you can believe something in your heart but if you don't act upon what you believe it will not manifest into faith.

There are many schools of thought that use the scripture, "faith without works is dead" to teach that we have to walk in works of faith that include taking ourselves off of medication, or not taking a child to a doctor or handing over a check when there's no money in your account. But a careful study of James chapter 2 from which he says three times, "faith without works is dead," will show that much of what James is referring to has to do with "speaking" and the examples of faith – and the works associated with that faith – have to do with "believing!" Verse 23 says, "and Abraham believed God."

The work of faith is speaking in faith that which you are hoping for! That's what the woman with the issue of blood did – she spoke, and continued to speak faith into her hopes of getting to Jesus, and touching his garment.

Speaking what you believe; believing what you know; knowing what you hear; and hearing and hearing the word of God is what will manifest and increase your faith in God – and in His word. These are the works of faith, and it is that faith that will manifest your healing!

And the best part about speaking this kind of healing into your life is that when you follow the example of the woman with the issue of blood, you can see that she created her own process for healing!

Based upon the scripture she knew, she determined for herself how her healing would come (through the hem of Jesus' garment), and when it would come (when she touched the hem of his garment). You too can know, believe, and speak the hope of your own healing into manifestation through faith in Jesus and His word of healing for you!

DO NOT DOUBT IT

Remember John 10:10 that says the thief comes not but for to steal, kill and destroy? Trust me, there is a very real thief, the enemy of your soul, the one who causes all sickness and disease, who does not want you to be healed! When you are trying to receive your healing the enemy will try to block it. That's why some healings seem "progressive." But when you do receive your healing, the enemy will try to reverse it. He will lie to you. He will try and continue to afflict your body and mind with the same symptoms, the same pains, and the same circumstances to make you think that your healing did not take. Do not doubt your healing!

This is where you must fight the good fight of faith! (1 Timothy 6:12) For many of us, doubt becomes a bastardized emotion when we use it to doubt God's truth in our lives. It will make our faith illegitimate and completely ineffective. Instead, we should doubt the doubt and the enemy's lies about God's truths for us. God wants you healed! God wants you well! God wants you whole! Never doubt it!

When the pain won't go away, do not doubt God's truth - keep speaking and declaring the word over your body. When the symptoms won't go away, do not fall prey to the doubt - continue speaking God's truth to the lies of the devil. When the doctor's tests still show the same results, do not give in to the facts, but keep standing on the truth of God. When family or friends keep speaking illness over you, reject the doubt that will try to creep into your resolve. And when you wake up each day, feeling the same, just declare again and again, today is the day of my healing!

I'm not saying it will always be easy. That's why scripture says to "fight" the good fight. Fighting does not imply "easy." And in fact, my own struggles and trials to be healed and efforts to maintain my divine healing have at times been extraordinarily difficult. Sometimes you can be sick for so long that your mindset knows nothing else. To "repent" means to change your mind, to turn away from. And sometimes it is so very difficult to repent from the mindset the devil has convinced us of regarding our health.

We've learned to manage diabetes through diet and insulin. We manage Hypertension through daily medication. We go through Chemo therapy and rejoice when tumors are shrinking. We lose a few pounds and settle for a certain weight when we've hit the doctor's goal for us. We're prescribed a medication that makes the migraine pain diminish in half the time as over the counter medication.

There are so many ways in which we have learned to live with the devil's lies for our lives and we justify it with many legitimate excuses such as:

- I'm not as bad off as I used to be
- It's just a natural part of growing old
- I'm doing better than many others my age
- Well, this condition runs in my family
- The doctor says I'll be fine so long as I take my meds
- My symptoms are getting better
- They've done all they can do/There's nothing else to do
- I'll just have to learn to live with it for the rest of my life
- I haven't had an attack in a long time
- I only get outbreaks once in a while so I'm doing better
- This time wasn't as bad as last time so I'm improving

We also have very good spiritual excuses and comments that the enemy uses against our healing and diving health as well such as:
- I'm standing on faith
- I know God can heal me
- Only Jesus is the healer
- All in God's timing
- Father knows best
- I'm believing for my healing
- I'm praying and hoping God will answer my prayers
- The church has prayed and they keep praying for me
- One day I'll see my healing
- Thank God for doctors because God uses them as His hands for healing

I've said it before - doctors are good and having a good doctor is even better! But doctors and medication are not God's divine best for our health and healing and in fact, even good doctors need God's divine best for their lives! God has a better way for your healing! Whether you are a doctor, nurse, pastor, social worker, mother, athlete or actor – God's way to pray for healing (for yourself and for others) is the best way! When you understand Mark 11:22-24, your healing is near!

The woman with the issue of blood took her own healing by faith. She made up her own mind how and when she was going to be healed. She determined if she touched the hem of His garment on that day that she pressed through the crowd, that she would be made whole – and indeed she was.

Jesus says to speak to our "mountain" and tell it what to do and how to do it. But all too often we still desperately pray and beg God to do something He's given us to do.

When we think of our own healing and try to apply the same application as the woman with the issue of blood, it might seem extraordinarily presumptuous to think we can make up our own mind how and when our miracle will be made manifest. In fact, when most believers actually try to apply this same process for healing as that woman did, they don't even get to the part about deciding for themselves how their healing will occur. Instead, we all immediately run into a very obvious snag that seems too difficult to unravel. How do we, not having access to Jesus here on earth any more, even touch the hem of His garment or the wings of His Talit?

Well, just like a knot that you might fuss around with trying to unravel, once you find that one loop, the rest seems to come easily undone. And so, the answer to this dilemma is the same. When we determine how to touch the hem of Jesus' garment in today's day and age, then we will be that much closer to being able to determine how and when we're healed.

John 1:1-4 says, "In the beginning was the Word, and the Word was with God, and the Word was God. The same was in the beginning with God. All things were made by him; and without him was not anything made that was made. In him was life; and the life was the light of men."

This Word is the Light of men that gives life – that's the same "Sun of Righteousness" that the woman with the issue of blood heard about from Malachi 4:2. But in John 1:14 it says that the Sun of Righteousness was made flesh. Well, actually it says that the Word, which was the Light of all men, "was made flesh, and dwelt among us, (and we beheld His glory, the glory as of the only begotten of the Father,) full of grace and truth." Jesus is the Word that became flesh – the very same Word that is the Light that lights all mankind.

Jesus is the Word who gives life; who wrapped Himself in the life, likeness and flesh of mankind – and yet He is still the Word, the Son of God who is and was God and was with God. Get it? Every time you read the word of God you are in the presence of Jesus. Every time you hear the word of God you are in the presence of Jesus. And every time you focus on the word of God that pertains to your healing and divine health, you are touching them hem of Jesus' garment! Have faith in the healing truth of God's word!

It's that faith in healing that will manifest your healing. And that is the faith you need to walk in the truth of Mark 11:22-24 that begins by saying "Have faith in God." Verses 23-24 go on to say: "For verily I say unto you, That whosoever shall say unto this mountain, Be thou removed, and be thou cast into the sea; and shall not doubt in his heart, but shall believe that those things which he saith shall come to pass; he shall have whatsoever he saith. Therefore I say unto you, What things so ever ye desire, when ye pray, believe that ye receive them, and ye shall have them."

When it comes to praying for your own healing or the healing of others the process according to these verses in Mark are the same – and they are similar to the process of the woman with the issue of blood:
1. Have Faith - Through hearing, knowing, believing, speaking & not doubting!
2. Speak to the mountain, problem, issue, sickness, disease, illness or infirmity
3. Tell it what to do ("Be removed")
4. Tell it how to do it ("Be cast into the sea")
5. Do not doubt what you've said to it
6. Believe that what you've said to it will come to pass

7. Expect to receive what you've spoken and that what you've spoken to will obey the words you've spoken!

You can do it and you must continue doing it. But it takes knowing the authority you have in Jesus – and in knowing the power of His name that He's given you. John 1:12 says you have the authority. Acts 1:8 says you have the power. Mark 16:15-16 says you have the ability. And John 15:7 gives you the same guarantee as Mark 11:14 that "If you abide in [Jesus], and [His] words abide in you, you shall ask what YOU will, and it shall be done unto you."

Ask, seek and knock on the door of your healing and you WILL receive whatever you ask! And if time goes beyond what you can bear – get tough, stay firm and stand on God's word!

Listen, in the beginning God gave all of mankind the stewardship, authority and dominion over this earth and all that is above it, on it or in the seas. (Genesis 1:26-28) Satan was (and is) jealous of that stewardship, authority and dominion and stole it away from Adam through Eve.

But God did not remove that stewardship, authority or dominion from mankind! And in that same Genesis blessing God also gave man the ability to SUBDUE the enemy in his attempts to steal, kill and destroy the stewardship, authority and dominion God has given us.

YOU have authority and dominion over the enemy and you have the power to subdue – to control, stop and put down his attacks over your life. Take your authority! Stand in your dominion by standing on God's word! You have the power to make satan stop raping your life through sickness, illness, depression and oppression! Speak your word of power and take back the power of your life like Proverbs 18:21 says!

LET'S GET HEALED:

THINK Healing...
Proverbs 23:7a – "As [a man] thinketh in his heart, so is he." Answer these few questions to ensure that you are thinking with a heart that believes in healing.

1.   What is God's will for your healing?

_____

_____

_____

2.   Does sickness come to teach you something; punish you for something?

   _____ YES   _____ NO

3.   Will Jesus heal today – in you and through you – the same as His ministry on earth?

   _____ YES   _____ NO

BELIEVE for Healing...
Choose three healing scriptures that speak to your heart regarding your healing. Write them below and memorize them. Meditate on them just as Joshua 1:9 says and then speak them every day along with this declaration of healing:

"My God is the same yesterday, today and forever and I know He wants me healed. Jesus made a way for my healing, as a part of my salvation. I know that as Jesus is, so am I in the world, therefore I am healed and made complete like Him."

Scripture #1:

_____

Scripture #2:

_____

Scripture #3:

_____

SPEAK Healing...
Mark 11:22-24 teaches us that when we speak **TO** something, believe it and do not doubt, it should obey. That means we are to speak directly to our pain, sickness or disease and tell it what to do and how to do it – then **believe** that it WILL obey!

RECEIVE Healing...
The prayers of the righteous availeith much! This is my prayer for your healing: "Father in Heaven, I thank you for each person reading this prayer. Father you know everything about each one. You know what their needs are and I thank you that you want them healed. Touch their hearts right now, ignite their faith and remove every obstacle and lie of the enemy that has kept them from the healing you have for them. I thank you and give you praise, in Jesus' name Amen."

5
Whole BODY...

Since the day of Adam and Eve's fall in the garden and their choice to walk into the judgment of God to eat of the Tree of the Knowledge of Good and Evil and die, mankind's physical bodies have been on an arc of birth to growth, growth to decline and decline unto death. For them, that decline to death lasted approximately 900+ years. For us in the 21 Century, we can hope that with good doctors, life-sustaining medicine and a healthy lifestyle perhaps we will extend our lives to 90 years, instead of 900.

But God has a different plan in mind for the lifespan of our physical bodies in this world – even with the fall of mankind and the decline of society and longevity after all these generations. Genesis 6:3 says we can have 120 years of life if we choose them. (And I do!) And so, we do not have to take "growing old" as just a normal part of life – even though it is. We do not have to expect certain ailments and issues simply because of age – even though they will most assuredly try to come. And we do not have to settle for the best the world has to offer in regards to doctors, medical research and breakthroughs in more effective medicines – even though yes, God will and does work through all of these things to bring about His healing.

God works through doctors because that's where our faith resides. Do not get me wrong – I am not saying "Don't go to a doctor" if you feel ill. I am not saying "If you do get ill, stop going to your doctor and rely on God." And I am not saying to "ignore the advice or medications of your doctor."

What I am saying is that Jesus never sent anyone to the doctor, and Jesus never had a case where He "attempted" to heal someone and was sued because it didn't work or a loved one died after taking His advice. Instead, those who did not believe or were too offended for faith to accomplish any more than a few miracles simply did not receive healing miracles. And I'm sure they continued with the practice of the day to see a physician and seek medical attention. But conversely, all who had a need, all who were brought to Jesus and all who touched Him or all whom He touched were healed – no doctors, no medicine and by no natural, reasonable methods.

You might say the profession of medicine was different then, and it was. However, Luke, the author of the book of Luke in the Gospels is referred to as "the Beloved Physician" in Colossians 4:14. However, Luke wrote about the healing miracles of Jesus more than any other biblical writer. And yet, even though he was a doctor himself, he never once had to clarify his writing, cover his "spiritual behind" and make the disclaimer that if you have doubts see a doctor, or do not ignore the advice of your doctor, or that God works through doctors.

All of these were as true then as they are today. However, Luke knew what I'm trying to get across to you – Jesus is God. God wants you well, and the proof is found in the healing miracles of Jesus. Jesus will heal YOU. Whether it is 15 BC or 2015 AD – Jesus is the Healer.

Unfortunately, throughout modern day history we hear (all too frequently) of the radical Believer in a certain sect of religious practice who:
- Died in childbirth because they wouldn't go to a doctor because of their faith
- Had a child die because they were trusting in God for that child's healing
- Suffered needlessly because their faith kept them from medical attention

None of these painful, tragic facts of today's society was ever sanctioned by God. I guarantee you the heart of God was grieved that again, the enemy was successful in stealing a life, and in these times he did so in the guise of faith and the blame was given to God. And equally as unfortunate is the depth of suspicion that is cast upon those vast multitudes in church history – both yesterday and rapidly more and more even today – who have received verified healings, miracle healings, creative healing miracles and who walk in divine health; healed by Jesus Christ.

Biblically, all those who had a need in their physical body, when they came to Jesus received. And just as the Word says, I believe Jesus is the same yesterday, today and forever (Hebrews 13:8). If Jesus lives in the life of the Believer then He is the same within that Believer as He was yesterday and as He will be forever.

Healing is not an accident or crazy whim of a fickle God whose heart we cannot know. Healing is not a divine lottery that we luck up upon if we are good or pray right. Unfortunately, there are many people who have passed on even when we've prayed in faith for their healing. But I say, blame the devil, not God or His divine process for healing!

When I received the revelation of just two scriptures, they became the ammunition I needed to command my healing and maintain ongoing health in my own body.

Galatians 3:13 – "Christ hath redeemed us from the curse of the law, being made a curse for us: for it is written, Cursed is every one that hangeth on a tree."

1 Peter 2:24 – "Who his own self bare our sins in his own body on the tree, that we, being dead to sins, should live unto righteousness: by whose stripes ye were healed."

I understood that when Jesus hung on that tree (the cross) for me, He did so much more than "just" provide a way for me to be forgiven of my sin and go to heaven. Jesus' death on the cross meant that I have the right to walk in healing and be redeemed from every attack or curse of the enemy against my health – my peace, my family, my life and prosperity too.

Deuteronomy 28:1-14 tells us about all the blessings God has for us. And while as Believers we get caught up in thinking that we can only receive those blessings if we are obedient to the Law and the commandments of God as it is written. But those truths were for the Jews, before Jesus. Now, because of Jesus' death on the cross, the blessings of Deuteronomy are ours – not because we earn them through our obedience to God but through Jesus' obedience to the cross. That's what Galatians chapter three says.

Now, not only are the blessings ours, but all those curses that are listed in Deuteronomy 28:15-68 cannot come near us. We are redeemed from every curse listed in that list. Not only that, but I determined we were also redeemed from the curse in the Garden as well. And every healing I might need that was associated with a curse, was what Jesus made provision for on the cross when He died for our sins.

Understanding these truths is one thing, but when revelation came, then these truths became a part of me. I knew that I was redeemed from every curse of conception from the Garden. I knew that no disease – whether I knew the name of it or not – could stay inside my body.

I knew that no sickness of a cold or flu, no headache, no allergy, not even poor eyesight could continue to distress me if I told it not to. And so, I began to speak to my body and tell it I was redeemed. Psalm 107:2 says, "Let the redeemed of the LORD say so, whom he hath redeemed from the hand of the enemy." Finally, I knew that all my ailments past, present and future were of the enemy and no matter what, I was (and am) forever redeemed through the blood of the Lamb of God.

This revelation - this knowledge - brought repentance. To "repent" is not to ask for forgiveness, it means to change your mind; to change your way of thinking and to turn away from in thought or belief. I had completely changed my way of thinking about healing and my own divine health!

And so the first thing I did with my new mind-set was to speak to the curse of conception in my body and tell it what to do. From the time I was thirteen years old I had consistently and painfully been wracked with the most excruciating menstrual cramps – every month – with fever, bowel issues and pain that was a 12 on the scale of 1-10!

But starting at the age of 45 I began to tell my body (and the enemy) that I was redeemed from the curse of the law and the curse of the Garden too. It took three months until one day – no cramps, no pain and no other symptoms. And the next month was the same and so on and so on.

And from then on, I decided what my body would and would not do. I got bold and I made the decrees – all by faith!

1. I decided I was done with needing glasses and wearing contacts. And so I was.
2. I decided I was done with seasonal allergies and sinus infections. And so I was.
3. I decided I was done getting colds and done with worrying about getting the flu. And so I was.
4. I decided that my weight could be managed through the word of God. And so it was.
5. And most of all, I've decided I will live until I'm 120 years old because the bible says I can. And so I will!

Headaches are now managed with a prayer, a command and a nap. Any sniffle is managed the same way. Severe and unexpected pain sometimes prove to be stubborn but generally within an hour and after a few forceful scripture commands that too would have to flee my body.

Any time someone tries to declare over me that certain ailments, issues and even weight gain are just a natural part of growing older and turning 50, I reject it and declare over myself that my heavenly Father is the one "Who satisfieth [my] mouth with good things; so that [my] youth is renewed like the eagle's. " Oh and, I'm not doing Menopause either!

Declaring this verse is what caused me to drop weight in three months, going from a size 9 to a size 6, without changing my eating habits, or increasing my exercise habit of walking each day. It is also the verse that surely keeps this fifty year old mother looking young enough to be carded when buying alcohol – depending upon what I wear.

God's word works. There is power in His word when it is mixed with faith. And it doesn't take loud faith; forceful faith; panicked faith or desperate faith. All it takes simple, mustard seed-sized, easy faith that **believes** the word of God.

But sometimes, even when you believe – or perhaps especially when you believe, the enemy will step up his game and force his hand against you even more – just to push your resolve and shake your faith. But I, like Jesus, pray your faith does not fail! Hold on to the word of God – and stay in belief.

I say this as emphatically as possible out of my own experience. I give you the testimonies of my own personal healings in order that your faith might increase. But I also want to share the truth of my struggles that your faith might not fail when the enemy pulls out all stops to trying to stop it.

At one point, not too long ago, the enemy began attacking my body from heel to head to the point where I had twelve different ailments and issues going on at the same time. I can't even say what pain or issue started first, but I do know that succumbing to them all began with migraines.

I was speaking against the "Richter scale 12" level pains in my heel that kept me limping, and in my elbow so that I was hindered from straightening my arm; as well as shortness of breath when I walked and an increase in weight of about 20 pounds! But when the migraines began I didn't have the physical, emotional or spiritual strength to fight them along with the other excruciatingly painful issues going on.

I'm sure many of you know when you have pain that severe on a daily basis you are frequently tired, irritable and weary. And so, when the migraines started, I took the Advil, said the prayer, made the command and took the nap. That's when the enemy began to have free reign and more power than I could pray or decree away with the word of God.

Don't misunderstand, it wasn't the Advil that caused the demise. It was the demise of faith and the fortitude to fight the good fight of faith that caused me to take the Advil.

Worst of all, the enemy was making statements against my faith through my attacks, and I knew exactly that he was!

1. Migraines attacked my mind-set and thinking
2. Blocked vision attacked my spiritual giftings
3. Tooth pain and blood blisters attacked my decrees
4. Neck & shoulder pain attacked my resolve
5. Heart weakness attacked my remission in the blood
6. A swollen elbow attacked my strength in the Lord
7. Weight gain attacked my balance and righteousness
8. Renewed cramping attacked my curse redemption
9. Irritable bowels attacked my flow in the Spirit of God
10. A blemish on my leg attacked my Christian walk
11. Plantar Fasciitis attacked my power to subdue attack
12. And depression attacked my peace of mind

Psalm 101:1-2 says, "I look to the hills from whence my help cometh, my help cometh from the Lord." And so I found my help in the word of God. Matthew 6:22 says that the eye is the light of the body and when the eye is single (clear and unwavering) then the whole body is full of light. And Isaiah 58:8 says, then, when your light is come, your health will spring forth speedily. However, refilling with light isn't easy!

I had to repent once again and return my thinking to the single-minded thought processes that determined God's word is true and every ailment in my body is a lie of the devil. It takes a faith fight to remember "I am redeemed; by His stripes I am made whole and Jesus the Healer lives in me!"

I had to put on the whole body, whole armor of God from Ephesians chapter 6 and remember that God has given me all the power and truth I need to combat the lies of the devil through the blood of Jesus and the Spirit of God who lives in me, quickens my mortal body and heals me – not because I earn it, but simply because He loves me dearly.

1 John 4:17 says, "Herein is our love made perfect; that we may have boldness in the day of judgement. Because as He is, so are we in this world." We are to be as Jesus in this world healed whole and powerful! And if Jesus said, "Have faith in God," then you can guarantee He had faith in God – of course He did! He came from the Father to give us the Father's name. That comes with more than just being able to call Yahweh, Adonai and El Shaddai our "Heavenly Father."

But like a child who grows and is respected in the family business because he has the father's name, or like a new wife who has access to her husband's bank account because she's taken on the last name – we too have been given a name that comes with authority and benefits. These include healing! Jesus is the name above every other name – and that includes the names of every disease, known and unknown!

Psalm 103:2-3 – "Bless the LORD, O my soul, and forget not all his benefits: Who forgives all thine iniquities; who heals all thy diseases;" As sure as you are about your salvation, you can be as equally sure of your healing! But you cannot succumb to the doubt, to the fear, to the ways and words of the world. Yes, your doctor may give you a diagnosis, and yes you may feel the pain still in your body, but Jesus is the name above any other name and that pain is the just the devil reminding you of what he's stolen from you for long enough! And Jesus has given you His name as power for your healing, deliverance, protection and so much more!

Get indignant! Get fired up! Get bold in your authority! Healing is your right, it's your benefit, it's the children's bread and you are a child of God! Have faith in God that He wants you well, He wants you healed and He wants you whole. Believe not only that God can, but that He WILL heal you!

Again, Mark 11:22-24 –"And Jesus answering saith unto them, Have faith in God. For verily I say unto you, That whosoever shall say unto this mountain, Be thou removed, and be thou cast into the sea; and shall not doubt in his heart, but shall believe that those things which he saith shall come to pass; he shall have whatsoever he saith. Therefore I say unto you, What things soever ye desire, when ye pray, believe that ye receive them, and ye shall have them."

When we apply these verses towards receiving our healing the practical steps look like this:

1. Have faith in God.
2. Speak to your body, the pain, disease, and issue
3. Tell it what to do ("be thou removed")
4. Tell it how to do it ("be thou cast into the sea")
5. Do not doubt in your heart
6. Believe that what you say will come to pass
7. Expect to receive what you've prayed for

I've said it repeatedly, it will not always be easy, although the word of God that I read makes me think that it should be. It will take commitment. It will take perseverance. It will take much diligence against the lies of the enemy, against the symptoms he will continue to bring, against the reports of the doctor and especially against your own mindset about your illness, pain or disease. But be encouraged Hebrews 11:6 says, "But without faith it is impossible to please him: for he that cometh to God must believe that he is, and that he is a rewarder of them that diligently seek him."

Be diligent as you continually seek God in faith for your healing! That's what is pleasing to God!

And don't be discouraged – you do have enough faith to continue believing in God, believing in His word, and speaking his word. And when you do, Romans 10:17 says, faith your faith will increase. But Romans 10:16 basically comes with a warning concerning your belief in God's word.

> **"But they have not all obeyed the gospel. For Esaias saith, Lord, who hath believed our report? So then faith cometh by hearing, and hearing by the word of God."**

I want you to believe this report. I want you to believe the word of God, and speak the word and continue to declare the word through whatever your body is telling you. God will reward you for your diligence just as He did mine! Faith in His word will increase as you continue to hear yourself speaking over your own body and speaking the word of God to your body and speaking to your body and telling it what to do and how to do it according to God's word.

The scriptures in Mark 11:22-24 come at the tail end of a bible story that may be familiar to you. Jesus and the disciples were coming from the town of Bethesda and Jesus was hungry. So, he saw a fig tree with leaves and went to it hoping to find figs. You see, I found out that this kind of fig tree produces figs at the same time it produces leaves. Well, there were no figs. That fig tree was lying. And Jesus "*answered* and said unto it, No man eat fruit of thee hereafter for ever. And his disciples heard it."

- Every pain in your body is your body speaking the devil's lie.
- Every symptom in your body is your body speaking a lie.
- Every illness in your body is your body speaking the devil's lie.
- Every disease in your body is your body speaking the devil's lie

- Every dis-ease, depression and distress in your body is your body speaking a lie!

God has given you the power of His word, and He's given you the power of faith – the measure of faith that He's given to *every* man – to answer those lies and speak the truth of God's word directly to every pain, symptom, illness, disease, dis-ease, depression and distress that you feel in your body! Your body may argue with you, but your own life and your own death are in the power of your own tongue! (Proverbs 18:21) Keep speaking the word of God!

And don't give up! Sometimes your body may not win the argument – especially in the beginning. And so you may have to relent and take the medication for a headache, or go to the doctor for that persistent cough. Whatever the case may be, do what you should in the natural and don't feel guilty until God builds you up in the supernatural. Believe for 100% supernatural healing, and declare 100% supernatural healing and expect 100% supernatural, immediately, suddenly and in that self-same hour healing results that Jesus manifested in his earthly ministry!

You see, Jesus wants to continue His earthly ministry in you and through you. As Believers we easily accept that Jesus lives in us. We understand that the Spirit of God lives in us. But what is far more difficult to understand is that Jesus wants to live **through** us and through our lives in the same manner that He lived through His own life! Yes, Jesus is The Healer, and His desire is to continue being that healer in your body and through your body, for the benefit of the Kingdom of God and to the Glory of God! When you do receive your healing, know that healing power is in you for the benefit of others too!

Jesus wants to heal you and He wants to heal others through you. In healing you, He will impart the anointing for and the ability heal unto you, to be a source of healing for others.

Matthew 28:18 is a very famous passage in which Jesus tells His disciples to go into all the world teaching and making disciples... this is what is known of in Christianity as "The Great Commission." However, what is not as well known is that in Mark's account of that same great commission, Jesus also said, "And as ye go, preach, saying, The kingdom of heaven is at hand. Heal the sick, cleanse the lepers, raise the dead, cast out devils: **freely ye have received, freely give**." (Mark 10:7-8)

If you have received your salvation, present that salvation to others. Many, many churches teach this as a natural part of evangelism that is a common expectation for every believer.

However, I believe that applies to other things too. If you have received teaching regarding the Kingdom of Heaven, present that teaching to others. And if you have been healed in your body, present that healing to others. Whatever God has freely given to you through the finished work of Jesus's death on the cross, you too can freely give it to others.

When Paul saw the impotent beggar at the Temple steps, he told him, "silver and gold have I none, but such that **I have, I give** unto you. Arise and walk." What did Paul give him? Healing in His body. And Paul said, "such that I have..." God wants you to receive your healing freely – without cost, without price. And that which you receive, you must also freely give. But giving healing doesn't start from a healing in your body it begins in the healing from your spirit.

6
Whole Body & SPIRIT…

When Adam and Eve disobeyed God and ate of the Tree of the Knowledge of Good and Evil God said in the day that they did, they would surely die. Well, we know that Adam and Eve did not drop down dead right then and there, but instead their spirits died.

That bond of Glory that covered them and connected them to God was severed and died in that day. And that spiritual death was passed on to every generation – as if eating from the forbidden tree gave them a terminal blood disease called "sin" that would always result in death. This disease was passed through the blood to every generation from Adam and Eve and could only be cured through the pure and holy blood of Jesus Christ and faith in Him.

And so, when you express your faith in Jesus, and confess that He is Lord and that God raised Him from the dead, you are then eating from the Tree of Life as God originally intended for all mankind. And just like the Tree of Life was to give Adam and Eve and all mankind eternal life (Genesis 3:22), we know that accepting Jesus as our Lord and Savior gives every man and woman eternal life as well.

John 3:16 is that famous verse that tells us this truth:

"For God so loved the world that He gave His only begotten Son that whosoever should believe on Him, shall not perish but have everlasting life."

That everlasting life is a result of the rebirth of your spirit. Jesus quickens you – or brings life unto the deadness of your spirit when you accept Him as your savior. And when your spirit is reborn it is reborn whole, complete and perfect with the mind of Christ. This is what scripture refers to as your "spirit man." But just like the "carnal man" – your natural body needs fuel and nourishment to thrive and grow.

When you read the word of God, hear the word of God and speak the word of God, your spirit man is given the fuel and the nourishment it needs for your soul to grow and mature in Christ! Remember 3 John 1:2 says, "Beloved, I wish above all things that thou mayest prosper, and be in health, even as thy soul prospers?" So how does your soul prosper? It prospers when it obeys your spirit!

1 Peter 1:22 says, "Seeing ye have purified your souls in obeying the truth through the Spirit unto unfeigned love of the brethren, see that ye love one another with a pure heart fervently:" And your soul can only obey the truth through the Spirit when your spirit is nourished by the Spirit of Truth through the study and understanding of God's word.

So how does all of this affect your healing? You know I've said you've got to do several steps for the healing of your body:
1. Hear it
2. Know it
3. Believe it
4. Speak it
5. Do not doubt it

But what is the "it" in all of these steps? Of course it is the word of God! I know I was clear that you have to hear the word of God; know the word of God; believe the word of God; speak the word of God and do not doubt the word of God when it comes to receiving healing in your body.

But that word can only get to your body when it is filtered through your soul and it can only get to your soul when it is filtered through your spirit. In fact, you can read the word with your mind (your soul) and not understand or receive a word of it. But when you mix it with faith you will receive that word through your spirit man and your soul and body must comply to the truth that your spirit knows!

When you are born again, you spirit is quickened (given life) and reborn. And your spirit is reborn in its perfect nature. Your born again spirit is whole, complete and perfect. Your born again spirit is holy. And, your born again spirit is seated in heavenly places in Christ Jesus.

The day your spirit is reborn, it becomes as perfect as it will ever be – for all eternity. Your spirit will not become more born again, more perfect or more complete once you die and go to heaven. In fact, your born again spirit is the link to a perfect heaven here on earth.

When we pray, "Our Father, which art in heaven, hallowed by thy name, thy Kingdom come, thy will be done, in earth as it is in heaven," we are praying the ability to bring heaven to earth! That is what God always intended for mankind to do – to be a link between heaven and earth and to manifest heaven on earth. And we do that through our spirit man. You need to know this because your spirit already knows what divine healing and wholeness really is!

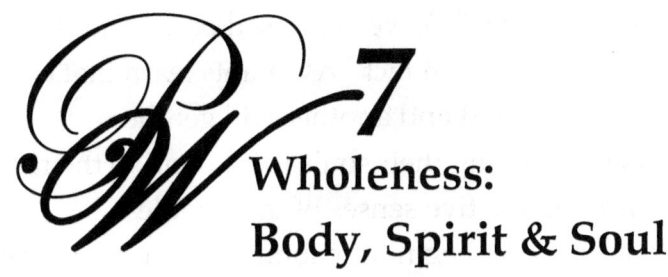

7
Wholeness: Body, Spirit & Soul

God is a spirit. And because we are created in His image and in His likeness we are a spirit too. In fact, when God breathed into the nostrils of Adam in the Garden it says that man became a living soul. God breathed the breath of His own Spirit into mankind in order for man to become a living soul. It is that spirit that died and is reborn when we're saved.

Therefore, you _are_ a spirit. You _have_ a soul and you _live in_ your body. Your spirit is how you are connected to, communicate with and interact with God. And your body is how you are connected to and communicate with and interact with the world. But your soul is the link between your spirit and your body. The Spirit of God speaks truth to your human spirit; your spirit then speaks this truth to your soul and your soul then speaks these truths to your body. Your body then should communicate all truth to the facts of this world, thereby manifesting your healing, health and prosperity.

When our bodies are wracked with disease, sickness and illness it is evidence of the fact that our bodies are influenced by the outside world and all that the enemy is able to attack us with through our five senses, and our feelings. Our bodies and souls are controlled by the world around us.

Unfortunately, from the day we are born, (with a spirit that is not quickened unto life), we are raised on an entirely different structure of truth and fact. As infants learn that a certain cry will get them fed and another will get them changed, they begin training their souls to respond to the facts of their world through the five senses of their bodies.

Soon enough we all begin functioning in our bodies by receiving the facts of the world through what we taste, smell, see, hear or feel. Then our bodies relay these facts to our souls; and these facts in our souls begin to make up the totality of who we think we are or our personalities. This is because our souls are our mind; will; emotion; intellect; experiences; memories and thoughts. And so, from the time we are born, all of who we think we are, what we know, and what we feel emotionally is a result of how we've processed the facts of the world into our souls through our five senses.

We grow up with our souls being in control of our bodies and the input received from the outside world. And once our spirit then is reborn – the battle begins for control! That's why scripture says that our soul should obey the truth from the Spirit – the Spirit that now speaks truth (not facts) to our soul.

Here is a chart of what it looks like when we are born again:

This is why 3 John 1:2 says that we prosper (in the world) and are in health (in our body) when our soul (our mind, will and emotions) prospers. Our soul prospers through the obeying of truth from the Spirit that is received through our spirit man. Our physical, natural prosperity and the prosperity of our divine health are in direct proportion to the prosperity of our souls!

So, if our soul is our mind, our will and our emotions – this means God wants you to prosper in your mental and emotional health as well! God wants to mend your broken heart, deliver you from the trauma of past experiences; free you from the bondage of depression and mental illnesses, and relieve you of all that distresses and stresses you out! You can be healed in your body as well as your mind!

- Be healed of fears!
- Be healed of insecurities!
- Be healed of depressions!
- Be healed of anxieties!
- Be healed of all confusion!

You can be made whole, body, spirit and soul! Psalm 107:8-9 says, "Oh, that men would praise the LORD for his goodness, and for his wonderful works to the children of men! For he satisfieth the longing soul, and filleth the hungry soul with goodness."

- If your soul is longing for peace, God will satisfy it
- If your soul is hungry for contentment, God will satisfy it
- If your soul is longing for joy, God will satisfy it
- If your soul is hungry for understanding, God will satisfy it
- If your soul is devoid of goodness in your life, God will fulfill it!

Scientists in the medical profession are determining that most physical diseases in our bodies are being caused by stress. Well, they are finally catching up with the truth of God's word! Psalm 107 also says that God will deliver us from our destructions, transgressions, iniquities, afflictions, distresses and diseases. And that means our dis-eases too!

Any mental illness, any depressive state of mind – manic or chronic; any aggressive state of mind; destructive state of mind; any adult ADD, ADHD or Autism, any chaotic state of mind and any other way in which our mind plagues us with a lack of peace can be healed and made whole through the word of God and the peace of Jesus that surpasses all understanding!

Do not take for granted the trauma of memories or experiences – like Post Traumatic Stress Disorder, (PTSD) as being an issue God can't do anything about. Too often Christians accept even just old age forgetfulness as a part of life we may have to deal with. And do not think of Dementia or Alzheimer's as being too hard for God. These issues are all attacks of the enemy against our souls!

Remember 3 John 1:2: "Beloved, I wish above all that you mayest prosper, and be in health, even as your soul prospers." God wants us all to prosper in our souls!

And, I want you to know, there is no disease – known or unknown that is too big for God. There is nothing that is so common unto man that God won't heal. Parkinson's; Stroke; Leukemia – whatever it is – every name of everything that the enemy can use to disrupt your health, peace and wholeness is still beneath the name of Jesus that is above every other name. There is power in the name of Jesus. Have faith in the name of Jesus and in the healing blood of the Lamb of God!

Jesus is our Shar Shalom – the Prince of Peace and that means there is peace for your mind. 2 Timothy 1:7 – "For God hath not given us the spirit of fear; but of power, and of love, and of a sound mind."

No matter what disturbs your mind, there is peace for it – and it's a peace that will drive out fear and it comes with power and love. In fact, 1 John 4:18 – "There is no fear in love; but perfect love casteth out fear: because fear hath torment. He that feareth is not made perfect in love." The love of Jesus will cast out the fear and torment disrupting your mind; and replace it with the mind of Christ that comes with power – the power to overcome the works of the devil! And Jesus, the Prince of Peace will manifest Himself to you through a sound mind and a prosperous soul!

God is our Jehovah Rophe – The Lord Who Heals. And He wants to heal you. As you begin to believe that, you will begin to see yourself, not just healed, but walking in divine health for the rest of your days with no fear of death. This is the grace of Jehovah Rophe for you, to...

1. Think of yourself as whole, because as a man thinks, so is he. (Proverbs 23:7)
2. Believe you can live a long, 120 years of life if YOU want to. (Genesis 6:3)
3. Remember, death is the last enemy of God and your enemy too! (1 Cor. 15:26)
4. And the power of your death and your life is in your tongue. (Proverbs 18:21)
5. If you desire to be well, it is God's delight to make you well. (Psalm 37:4)

In John 14:6 Jesus says, "I am the way, the truth, and the life: no man cometh unto the Father, but by me." And when you come to the Father by way of Jesus, you will find that Jesus is The Way to your healing. Jesus is The Truth for your divine health. And Jesus is your abundant, prosperous, eternal, everlasting, very long and perfectly whole Life!

God wants you to prosper and be in health and Jesus wants you well. And when you touch the heart of the Spirit of the Lord for your healing you too will be like those in Matthew 14:36, who sought out Jesus, "And besought him that they might only touch the hem of his garment: and as many as touched were made perfectly whole."

As you have been reading the truth of God's word, you have touched the hem of Jesus' garment through these pages. They were written with the Spirit of the Lord being present for YOUR healing. As I said, God's truth and power is able to transcend space and time – because He is outside of time. God knew who would be reading this and when you would be reading and His desire is that you are healed and made whole through what you have read.

Luke 9:11 says, "And the people, when they knew it, followed him (Jesus): and He received them, and spake unto them of the kingdom of God, and healed them that had need of healing." The word "gospel" means "too good to be true news," and the gospel for you is that God wants you healed!

Can you hear the Kingdom truth of God's gospel message of healing for you? If you can, then that is the heartbeat of God for your healing and divine health. It is a steady rhythm of His love for you, tapping out the beat of His Kingdom, and His divine truth that says you can be made perfectly whole: body, spirit and soul.

LET'S GET WHOLE:

THINK Wholeness…
Philippians 4:8 "Whatsoever things are true, honest, just, pure, lovely, good report; virtuous and if there be any praise, think on these things." When sick, you have to think yourself whole!

1. How do you know whether God wants you whole?

_____

_____

2. Will God restore all things related to your healing that are separate from your health when you are made whole?

   ____ YES   ____ NO

3. Are healing, long life, peace, abundance and wholeness a part of your salvation through Jesus Christ?

   ____ YES   ____ NO

BELIEVE in Wholeness…
Choose three bible accounts of wholeness that will ignite your faith to be made completely whole. Meditate on them daily and determine that long life and divine health is a part of your inheritance in Jesus Christ. Believe God's word and speak this declaration each day as a part of maintaining your healing, walking in perfect health and being made perfectly whole.

"I receive my healing and declare that I walk in divine health. I am redeemed from every curse of the law and that includes sin, sickness, disease and death. I will walk in perfect wholeness and complete peace for all my 120 years: nothing missing, lacking or broken in Jesus name!"

Scripture #1:

_____

Scripture #2:

_____

Scripture #3:

_____

SPEAK Wholeness...
Matthew 21:22 tells us that when we pray, we will receive that which we believe. Speak your prayers and believe that when you pray you have already received all you are praying for!

RECEIVE Wholeness...
This is my prayer for your divine health and wholeness: "Oh, Heavenly Father – Thank you for all who are reading this and come before you in agreement with me right now. I speak to every disease known and unknown that it cannot prevail in their bodies and no weapon formed against them shall prosper. I speak life to their flesh and healing to their bones. Let all things work decently and in order and be in balance, that they be made perfectly whole in Jesus' name, Amen."

Jesus...

"Surely he hath borne our griefs, and carried our sorrows: yet we did esteem him stricken, smitten of God, and afflicted. But he was wounded for our transgressions, he was bruised for our iniquities: the chastisement of our peace was upon him; and with his stripes we are healed" – Body, Spirit & Soul...
   Isaiah 53:4-5

May ALL of God's blessings always be yours,
~Pastor Deidre Campbell-Jones

Pastor Deidre Campbell-Jones is the head of the non-denominational, 7-M Kingdom Congregation, The House of His Glory in Sylmar, CA.

The House of His Glory is a Kingdom, Power and Glory congregation that believes church is not a place to go or a thing to have, but that The Church is who we are: A Church doing great and greater works for the Kingdom of Heaven; with the power of Jesus Christ and to the Glory of God!

You are invited to join this ministry and learn to walk in the fullness of all God has purposed you to do; have all that Jesus died on the cross for you to have and be exactly who God created you to be – the Church of Jesus Christ, His Bride, to be presented to Him without spot or blemish upon the day of His soon coming return.

Visit Pastor Deidre and The House of His Glory eMinistry through http://www.iChurch4Life.com. Also, you can download the "ichurch4life" App available on Google Play and the Apple Store.

Contact us for leadership training and resources, or to establish a ministry under the covering of Bishop Jason L. Sample and Pastor Deidre Jones.

Power, Love & Peace –
~*Pastor Deidre Campbell-Jones, M.Th.*

The House of His Glory
www.iChurch4Life.com

www.ingramcontent.com/pod-product-compliance
Lightning Source LLC
Chambersburg PA
CBHW071410040426
42444CB00009B/2187